The Paper Playlist
Exploring the Power of Music Therapy

George Cooper

DEDICATION

This book is dedicated to you.

THE PAPER PLAYLIST: THE POWER OF MUSIC THERAPY

CHAPTERS

	How to use QR Codes	6
1	Motivation & Exploration	7
1.5	Send This To A Friend	28
2	Zone Out	38
3	Profound Lyrics	69
4	Hype Me Up	90
5	In My Feels, Yearning For You	115
6	In My Feels F**k You!	146
7	Sunday	176

INTRODUCTION

Have you felt need to, express your feelings, turn your dreams into reality or to simply find the right words to say? Have you ever wanted to find love, tell someone how you really feel or just take some time out for yourself? If so, this is the book for you.

The Power of Music is spectacular & can move you physically, spiritually & emotionally.
Whether this is down to the lyrics or the arrangement of chords. Songs create a feeling you cannot explain.

My purpose for this book is to help you find the peace I found within myself. Let you in on songs that have helped me throughout my journey and every single emotion I have had to endure. Life is very unpredictable & can change at any point.

Reading a new quote, having conversations with family and friends, or even a stranger. Can make a significant difference towards your journey called 'life'.
The greatest and most profound quotes come from a place of healing & perspective.

This is how 'The Paper Playlist' came to life. I believe music is therapy & so are shared experiences. This book is a perfect blend of the two.

Throughout the book, there will be eight Chapters. Each chapter reflects a mood or a feeling. Alongside each quote there will be a QR code to scan. This QR code will link you to a song to help delve into the quote even further or simply add a new song to your discography.

I hope this book helps you, as much as it has me writing it.

HOW TO USE QR CODES

APPLE MUSIC – To listen to the song, simply open your camera app & point your camera over the QR Code.

This will instantly link you to the song.

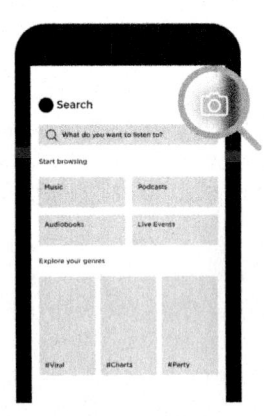

SPOTIFY – To listen to the song, open the 'spotify' app.

Select 'search' tab.

Select the camera icon on the top right of the screen.

SPOTIFY – STEP 2

Point the camera over the 'spotify' QR code.

Your song will instantly play.

CHAPTER ONE
MOTIVATION & EXPLORATION

"We should not measure success by bank accounts
filled with money,
but rather by moments filled with joy and gratitude.

Pursuing your passion vigorously and relentlessly will bring
you those moments." — Dennis Houchin

MOTIVATION & EXPLORATION

"Promise yourself,
to accept life as it comes
and truly make each day special.

    To become more independent and more willing to change.
    To fill your life with special times,
    and make your dreams come true" – Deanna Beisser

MOTIVATION & EXPLORATION

"You become what you surround yourself with.
Energies are contagious.
Choose carefully.
Your environment will become you. "

MOTIVATION & EXPLORATION

"There are people waiting to meet you. People waiting to love you. There are places that stand still until you've stepped foot in them. Something really beautiful could happen for you in the morning. There is so much waiting for your arrival, arrive there." – Brianna Pastor

MOTIVATION & EXPLORATION

"If you practice gratitude,
it makes sense of our past,
brings peace for today
and creates
a vision for tomorrow."

MOTIVATION & EXPLORATION

"Pay close attention
to all the ways you unintentionally taught people
how to treat you.
By being available for them,
putting their problems before your own.
Sacrificing your personal time to help them or
keep them company.
If you can go to bed knowing you've done something
 for someone else,
no matter how big or small.
You will sleep better."

MOTIVATION & EXPLORATION

"As you become more you,
you'll become less you,
in the eyes if certain people....
its not your responsibility
to keep up with versions of you
that they want to see."

THE PAPER PLAYLIST: THE POWER OF MUSIC THERAPY

MOTIVATION & EXPLORATION

"Stop hating yourself for everything you aren't,
start loving yourself for everything you already are. "

MOTIVATION & EXPLORATION

"Learn to realize
its not about changing the world,
it's about realizing
you are the world. "

Pick yourself up, blast this song – it's a classic!

THE PAPER PLAYLIST: THE POWER OF MUSIC THERAPY

MOTIVATION & EXPLORATION

"Make decisions from the perspective of who you want to become.

A wrong decision is better than an indecision.

"The magic you are looking for, is in the work you're avoiding." - Chris Williamson

THE PAPER PLAYLIST: THE POWER OF MUSIC THERAPY

MOTIVATION & EXPLORATION

"Sometimes, your old life has to fall apart
before your new life can fall together.
So, don't hesitate to leave the past in the past."

THE PAPER PLAYLIST: THE POWER OF MUSIC THERAPY

MOTIVATION & EXPLORATION

"Fear is an invitation to evolve, the world is as you are.
Don't compare.
There are people out there
who have never experienced 'struggle'.
Can you imagine not knowing any different?
How do they appreciate their wins..
when they have been winning? "

Read that again & play this track.

MOTIVATION & EXPLORATION

"The people who need the most love,
ask for it in the most unloving ways.
Make that commitment to yourself,
to no longer ask for love un-lovingly,
communicate about the type of love you need
in an open & honest way.

Rather than hoping that someone else
is going to figure it out, on its own.
Stop being distant,
Stop sending subliminal messages
Stop avoiding the talk."

MOTIVATION & EXPLORATION

"Today is a new day, tomorrow is never promised.
Approach today with gratitude for yourself and others.
You are a gift.
Life is a gift.
Be open and understand every day has many possibilities,
every moment is precious.
Every choice is meaningful & serves its purpose."

MOTIVATION & EXPLORATION

"We are who we are, when nobody's watching, if you wanna know who you really are, be on your own, go somewhere on your own, go on holiday with yourself or whatever and that's who you are. If you're driving along & you throw the soda can out of the window of the car. That's who you really are. No one does that with kids in the back, "Monster".. but if you do that, if that's who you are, its interesting to note that. Its the difference between character and reputation. You really know who you are, "reputation is what everyone else thinks about you. But you really know who you are in yourself." - Jimmy Carr

MOTIVATION & EXPLORATION

The Beatles, "Hey Jude" is about
gaining courage,
overcoming shyness
and fear, and going out there
to get the love you have found.

So, what are you waiting for?

MOTIVATION & EXPLORATION

Listen to this song as you read this.

"I'm so proud of you for doing your best to be okay. I'm so proud of you for waking up everyday and trying. If you change your mind a million times, that's okay. If you change your job a million times, that's okay. Life hands you many options for you to choose from. I don't know what your going through, but you are going to get through it. I hope you fight for yourself when no one else does. I hope you know how worthy you are of your wildest dreams. You are someone worth fighting for, keep going!"

MOTIVATION & EXPLORATION

"When you're not used to being confident. Confidence will feel like arrogance. When you're used to being passive, assertiveness will feel like aggression. When you're not used to getting your needs met, prioritizing yourself feels selfish. With all that being said, your comfort zone is not always a good benchmark."

MOTIVATION & EXPLORATION

"What if its happening, exactly how its supposed too? What if its working out better than expected? What if you're right on schedule? What if you weren't supposed to be with that person? What if this is the best thing that's ever happened to you, and you don't even know it yet?

Play in the realm of possibility. I don't even know what's going to happen next, but I know in my heart & soul. Trust the process, because its going to be even better than what was passed. More aligned, more fulfilling... better in every single way." Be Hopeful

MOTIVATION & EXPLORATION

Chris Williamson – The lonely chapter.

"There is a period in everybody's journey where, they are so different., because they have started to do new things but they no longer fit in with the old set of friends but they're not sufficiently developed that they've gained their new set of friends.

They're unsure.. "Should I go back, should I lean-back into getting a bag in with the boys on the weekend, is that the highest way that I can live my life? Passion forward. Because that's what everybody else does?
All of my friends are taking the p**s;
*"Oohhhh not drinking again, too good for us are we…Not going out again this week? Oh okay well enjoy staying in at home and reading f**king nerd."*

So you are going to feel the pain of being ostracized by friends that you used to have..but you're stuck in this messy middle. Where you haven't yet worked out who you are on the other side of this & that lonely chapter that's in the middle is something that. I would say that almost nobody that I've ever met.. who has gone from a place where they are to a place where they want to be.. *hasn't* gone through"

THE PAPER PLAYLIST: THE POWER OF MUSIC THERAPY

CHAPTER ONE.FIVE

SEND THIS TO A FRIEND

"There is something so beautiful about having long-term friends, that have witnessed multiple versions of you and loved you unconditionally through each version."

THE PAPER PLAYLIST: THE POWER OF MUSIC THERAPY

SEND THIS TO A FRIEND

"Be nice to your mum,
its her first time living life too."

THE PAPER PLAYLIST: THE POWER OF MUSIC THERAPY

SEND THIS TO A FRIEND

" For as long as I exist. You will always be loved."

THE PAPER PLAYLIST: THE POWER OF MUSIC THERAPY

SEND THIS TO A FRIEND

" If you and your cousins,
didn't choreograph a dance together,
did y'all even have a bomb ass childhood."

Send some love to your favorite cousin!

SEND THIS TO A FRIEND

" Breath darling this is just a chapter."

"Its not your whole story. In order for something new to come. Something old must go and that old can sometimes mean.. Let go. Of what you know, until now.

Empty the cup & start from the beginning.

Its not easy to do, but its the only way that has been blocked can be brought back to movement.

Spill out the old tea & pour a new one" – Mulligan Brothers

THE PAPER PLAYLIST: THE POWER OF MUSIC THERAPY

SEND THIS TO A FRIEND

"We should certainly count our blessings,
      but we should also make our blessings count."

SEND THIS TO A FRIEND

"Oh the comfort the inexpressible comfort of feeling safe with a person of neither having to weigh your thoughts nor measure your words. That is friendship"– George Elliot

SEND THIS TO A FRIEND

"If you're stuck on a problem,
don't sit there & think about it;
just start working on it.

Even if you don't know what you're doing,
the simple act of working on it will eventually
cause the right ideas to show up in your head.
The desire for the positive experience is itself a negative experience."

THE PAPER PLAYLIST: THE POWER OF MUSIC THERAPY

SEND THIS TO A FRIEND

"Throughout life we experience many different kinds of friendships. On rare occasions, we encounter someone so special that we just know we met for a reason. These are the kinds of friendships that last forever no matter what city you live in or how often you speak, no matter how old you get or what phase of life you are in. Its the type of friendship that has no judgment and sticks by you even when you f*ck up. Its the kind of friendship that makes you understand unconditional love. Maybe you met your most special friend when you were 6 or 13 or 30… or maybe you are yet to cross paths. It happens at different stages for different people. But when it does there is no greater comfort than knowing that this person will be right there beside you to share happiness, the sadness & everything in-between. Never, ever take these friendships for granted" - Charlotte Freeman – **book**: *Everything you'll ever need.*

THE PAPER PLAYLIST: THE POWER OF MUSIC THERAPY

SEND THIS TO A FRIEND

"I just want to tell you that,
    talking to you was
        one of the best parts of my whole year." -

SEND THIS TO A FRIEND

"Your purpose in life is not to love yourself, but to love *being* yourself. If your goal is to love yourself, then your focus is directed inward towards yourself.

You end end up consistently watching yourself from the outside, disconnected trying to summon the correct feelings towards yourself or fashion yourself into something you can approve of.

However if your goal is to love being yourself then your focus is directed outward, towards life.

On living and making decisions based on what brings you pleasure & self-fulfillment.

'Be the Subject and not the Object.

It doesn't matter what you think of yourself, you are experiencing life and life is not experiencing you."

SEND THIS TO A FRIEND

The person who sent you this, wants you to know..

"I literally don't know how you do it all.
You're one of the bravest and strongest people I've ever known. I'm so proud of you and I just wanted to remind you
I care about you so much.
Please take care of yourself a little extra today.
Do whatever you need to do to be okay.
You're doing better than you think."

SEND THIS TO A FRIEND

"Chaos is inevitable, Loss is inevitable. It is not the pain or the problem, that is actually the problem. It is your reaction to the problem or situation that is causing our suffering.

The pain can only exist for so long in your body but the meaning and the stories that we put to the pain continue the "hamster wheel" of suffering. There is a Buddhist saying that pain is inevitable but suffering is optional.

The sooner that you can accept and find peace in every situation, the sooner you are freed from the suffering you're experiencing"

SEND THIS TO A FRIEND

"Life doesn't give you the people you **want**.
It gives you the people you **need**.
The people that are going to hurt you, the people who are gonna love you & that are going to make you question.. who you want to be?

That is absolutely terrifying, but you have to learn to be completely okay with it because there's no other way around it.

After all this whole story that we are living is about finding yourself. Not about finding somebody else. The rest fits in, naturally."

THE PAPER PLAYLIST: THE POWER OF MUSIC THERAPY

SEND THIS TO A FRIEND

"Life is Short, You get 4,000 weeks if you're lucky. Book that flight. Apply for that job. Start that business & ask that person on a date! Stop limiting your self. Lead with love & play this song."

SEND THIS TO A FRIEND

"Queer people don't grow up as ourselves., we grow up playing a version if ourselves that sacrifices authenticity to minimize humiliation and prejudice, the massive task of our adult lives is to unpick which parts of ourselves are truly us, and which parts were created to protect us."

SEND THIS TO A FRIEND

"Before you go to bed tonight.
I want you to remember
that it took a lot of courage to leave behind,
what's not for you any-more.

If you're strong enough to let go, then you'll be strong enough to find what's next for you.

You've got this, goodnight."

SEND THIS TO A FRIEND

"People are people, non of its intentional, never attribute to malice by contributing to incompetent its far more likely, that they're all in their own worlds, doing their own thing, they're not paying attention to the world around them. We all do it everyday, whether you're driving, walking down the street all of our lives is just as complex as everybody else's.

Everything you think you have going on, they have it going on. Nobody knows what everybody else is going through. We also need to be a little it more self-aware and aware of the world around us."

THE PAPER PLAYLIST: THE POWER OF MUSIC THERAPY

SEND THIS TO A FRIEND

"You don't always get the closure you want, but you will always get the outcome you need. Everything happens for a reason, everything that hurts, shall pass." - Drake

SEND THIS TO A FRIEND

Did you know, that everyday the heart creates enough energy to drive a truck 20 miles?
In a lifetime that is equivalent to driving to the moon and back..
So when you say to someone,
you 'Love them to the moon & back'

you're essentially saying to them
that you love them with all the blood
that your heart pumps your entire life.

When you next say this line, just remember what it means.

With that being said. "I love you to the moon & back."

CHAPTER TWO
ZONE OUT

Try not to overthink, close your eyes,
play this song & just vibe.

ZONE OUT

"Being alone doesn't mean being lonely;
being alone does not make you weak.
It means you're strong enough to wait for what you deserve

.. be patient.

Your progress does not need to be seen or validated by others to be real.
You are on your own unique journey.
Spend some time with yourself recharge & re-evaluate
so you can be present with your future self..
with making memories,
building friendships,
 marching for what you believe in,
exploring new places &
just being there for the people who mean the most.
You'll thank yourself later." – @georgethemillenial

ZONE OUT

Do you ever find yourself,
          staring into the abyss?
    Cut off from your daily commitments,
      play this song & get lost in your own thoughts.

I've spent hours just thinking about possibilities,
      with that one person..
         Or multiple...
             No judgment here.

THE PAPER PLAYLIST: THE POWER OF MUSIC THERAPY

ZONE OUT

If its cold outside & you want to sit, wrap up & have a nice hot drink...Be sure to play this.

ZONE OUT

"When you learn to enjoy your own company, you become less reliant on external validation and find true contentment within"

ZONE OUT

"Let go of the tension, let go of the worries. Surrender to the present moment & feel it.
Turn up the volume for this one."

THE PAPER PLAYLIST: THE POWER OF MUSIC THERAPY

ZONE OUT

"Find your own oasis of peace & make time to escape into it regularly. Play this song & practice this."

ZONE OUT

"Find your sanctuary, whether it's in nature, a cozy nook, or the pages of a good book, and let rest envelop you. Unplug, unwind, and disconnect from the chaos; this chapter is found in simplicity."

ZONE OUT

"Loneliness is a kind of tax you have to pay to atone for a certain complexity of the mind "– Alain de Botton

ZONE OUT

Take care of your mind,
"There is virtue in work and there is virtue in rest. Use both and overlook neither." - Alan Cohen

ZONE OUT

if you had a friend,
    who spoke to you
in the same way,
    that you spoke about yourself..
        How long would you allow this person
            to be in your life?

ZONE OUT

"Surrender to what is.
　　　Let go of what was.
　　　　　　Have faith in what will be." - Sonia Ricotti

ZONE OUT

"Trust the path you're on.
Sometimes it may seem uncertain,
but every step is guiding you toward your purpose."

ZONE OUT

"Engage in daydreaming:
Allow your mind to wander freely and indulge.

Let your thoughts drift without any particular goal or agenda."
Relax your eyes & let the song move you.

ZONE OUT

"Inhale peace,
exhale stress;
this chapter begins with a breath & a good song."

THE PAPER PLAYLIST: THE POWER OF MUSIC THERAPY

ZONE OUT

"Sometimes, you have to forget about your responsibilities, give yourself a couple of minutes, zone out & reset.

ZONE OUT

It's okay to have a cry to yourself, you know.
Research has found that in addition to being self-soothing, shedding emotional tears releases oxytocin and endorphins.
These chemicals make people feel good and may also ease both physical and emotional pain.
In this way, crying can help reduce pain and promote a sense of well-being.

ZONE OUT

"Find your own rhythm of relaxation,
whether it's through nature,
music,
meditation,
or simply being present in the moment."

THE PAPER PLAYLIST: THE POWER OF MUSIC THERAPY

ZONE OUT

Let these melodies transport you to a state of tranquility.

ZONE OUT

'Carpe Diem' - "seize the day"

CHAPTER THREE
PROFOUND LYRICS

"I think it's time to kill for our women, Time to heal our women, be real to our women And if we don't we'll have a race of babies, That will hate the ladies that make the babies"
- Tupac Shakur

THE PAPER PLAYLIST: THE POWER OF MUSIC THERAPY

PROFOUND LYRICS

"Tell me who I have to be to get some reciprocity? No one loves you more than me, and no one ever will." - Lauryn Hill

PROFOUND LYRICS

"I am no longer trying to survive,
 I believe that life is a prize
  But to live, doesn't mean you're alive."
   – Nicki Minaj

PROFOUND LYRICS

"What's the problem with the world today? The land of the free, somebody lied." —Prince

THE PAPER PLAYLIST: THE POWER OF MUSIC THERAPY

PROFOUND LYRICS

"Reach for the stars so if you fall...you land on the clouds."

- Ye West

PROFOUND LYRICS

"You're so much better than you know, When you're lost and you're alone, And you can't get back again, I will find you, Darling, and I will bring you home- Sade

THE PAPER PLAYLIST: THE POWER OF MUSIC THERAPY

PROFOUND LYRICS

"May you grow up to be righteous. May you grow up to be true. May you always know the truth, and see the light surrounding you. May you always be courageous, stand upright and be strong. May you stay forever young."
– Bob Dylan

PROFOUND LYRICS

I've been a victim of, A selfish kind of love, It's time that I realize, That there are some with no home, Not a nickel to loan, Could it be really me, Pretending that they're not alone? – Michael Jackson

PROFOUND LYRICS

"So even if I could wouldn't go back where we started, I know you're still waiting wondering where my heart is, Pray that things won't change but the hardest part is, You're realizing maybe I, maybe I ain't the same."
- Olivia Dean

THE PAPER PLAYLIST: THE POWER OF MUSIC THERAPY

PROFOUND LYRICS

"How you feel about the way your life is goin'?
And tell me why you'd wanna go through it alone, hey

Won't you live for me?
Or could I live for you?
There's nothing I won't carry
So you don't have to "
       – Omar Apollo

THE PAPER PLAYLIST: THE POWER OF MUSIC THERAPY

PROFOUND LYRICS

"This like a game of survival,
why am I dying for a title?

Is it even worth the fight? When ill just end up alone" – SiR

PROFOUND LYRICS

"My frequency's seamless
They want you give more, expect you to dream less
Got me confessin' all my secrets
You ain't the only one under deep stress
Please, don't take my kindness for a weakness
Get G-checked for your disrespect
Perception and observation is clinical
More headspace, I've been shavin' off my occipital
They say, "You can't hate who you don't love"
And they say, "Love is unconditional"
I'm ready to do the unthinkable
Fuck rules and everything that's traditional
Giving your heart to someone might just leave you in a somethin',"

- Little Simz

THE PAPER PLAYLIST: THE POWER OF MUSIC THERAPY

PROFOUND LYRICS

" I like it in the city when two worlds collide, You get the people and the government, Everybody taking different sides" – Adele

THE PAPER PLAYLIST: THE POWER OF MUSIC THERAPY

PROFOUND LYRICS

"Oh, thunder only happens when it's raining, Players only love you when they're playing, Say, women, they will come and they will go, When the rain washes you clean, you'll know

– Fleetwood Mac

PROFOUND LYRICS

"Don't gain the world and lose your soul, Wisdom is better than silver and gold." - Bob Marley

THE PAPER PLAYLIST: THE POWER OF MUSIC THERAPY

PROFOUND LYRICS

"Keep me in your mirror
But don't take your eyes off the road
Holding on won't get us any nearer
'Cause we got a long way to go
Sometimes it's hard to see
That some things just won't be" – Madison Ryann Ward

PROFOUND LYRICS

"I believe that children are our future. Teach them well and let them lead the way. Show them all the beauty they possess inside." - Whitney Houston

THE PAPER PLAYLIST: THE POWER OF MUSIC THERAPY

PROFOUND LYRICS

"We could have been so good together, We could have lived this dance forever, But now, who's gonna dance with me? Please stay.

I'm never gonna dance again, Guilty feet have got no rhythm, Though it's easy to pretend, I know you're not a fool"

– George Micheal

PROFOUND LYRICS

"War is not the answer, because only love can conquer hate."

- Marvin Gaye

PROFOUND LYRICS

"I don't care if they give me life
I get all of my life from you
And if loving you had a price
I would pay my life for you

I hear sirens while we make love
Loud as hell but they don't know
They're nowhere near us
I will hold your heart and your gun
I don't care if they come, no
I know it's crazy but I don't care I'll never give it up" - Beyoncé

Deeper then words, beyond right
Die for your love, beyond life
Sweet as a Jesus piece, beyond ice
Blind me, baby, with your neon lights
Ray Bans on, police in sight
Oh, what a beautiful death
Let's both wear white
If you go to heaven and they bring me to hell
Just sneak out and meet me, bring a box of L's
She fell in love with the bad guy
- Jay Z

CHAPTER FOUR
HYPE ME UP

If you are at a pre-drinks before your night out & you don't know what to queue on the speaker.

Queue this, it never misses.

HYPE ME UP

"Surround yourself with the best circle of friends,
for they are the mirrors reflecting your true potential.

Can't nobody f**k with your clique."
This song is the definition!

HYPE ME UP

"True friendship is forged in the fires of shared laughter, dance, and celebration our wins!"

Blast this song with your friends and party.

# HYPE ME UP

This classic will go down in history for one of the most illuminating Bashment/Dancehall songs. Period.

HYPE ME UP

At any opportunity,
        this song can hype a crowd at any event,
                any party or wedding.

Listen to the lyrics from both perspectives.

Lauryn you are a legend.

THE PAPER PLAYLIST: THE POWER OF MUSIC THERAPY

HYPE ME UP

Whether it's a rooftop bar or a summer garden BBQ, songs like this hit your soul.

Its essential for the soul's well-being, a reminder that we are alive and kicking in the grand symphony of life.

HYPE ME UP

Outside of her controversial statements.

Azealia Banks has undeniably left a significant mark on the queer house music scene.

Her electrifying tracks and unapologetic persona have resonated deeply with the LGBTQ+ community and beyond. Her fearless exploration of her own sexuality and identity, coupled with her eclectic musical style, has provided a bold voice for queer expression within the house music scene.

The fearless artistry and fierce advocacy have helped break down barriers, fostering a more inclusive and liberated atmosphere within the world of house music, where individuality and authenticity reign supreme.

I can speak for many, Azealia we thank you.

HYPE ME UP

Caribbean dancehall music has undeniably left an indelible mark on the global music industry, resonating with audiences far beyond its island origins.

Its infectious rhythms, bold lyrics, and distinctive sound have infiltrated various music genres, shaping the sonic landscapes of hip-hop, pop, and electronic music.

Additionally, dancehall's flamboyant fashion and vibrant dance moves have inspired fashion trends and choreography in music videos and live performances, amplifying its cultural impact. Beyond the music itself.

This song has not only carved out a significant niche within the music industry but has also helped bridge cultures, fostering a dynamic and inclusive global musical tapestry.

HYPE ME UP

Letting go of your inhibitions and partying until the sun rises is an exhilarating journey into the depths of freedom and self-expression.

As the night unfolds, the music pulses through your veins, the dance floor becomes a canvas for your wildest moves, and laughter fills the air as you connect with newfound friends. In these precious moments, societal norms and worries vanish into the darkness, and you become a part of something greater, a symphony of life in full crescendo.

As the first rays of dawn break the horizon, you're left with unforgettable memories and a reminder that sometimes, it's essential to embrace the night and dance until the world is reborn with the morning sun.

THE PAPER PLAYLIST: THE POWER OF MUSIC THERAPY

HYPE ME UP

"In the art of dancing, we celebrate the beauty of the present moment, for it is in the dance that we truly live."

HYPE ME UP

"Raves are more than just parties; they are spaces where we find freedom, self-expression, and a sense of belonging in the rhythm of the night.

Dance like there's no tomorrow, we discover the joy of existence."

HYPE ME UP

Robin S – 'Show me Love' is one of the most iconic dance songs ever written.

There wouldn't be much point in me including this song in the book because I'm sure you've already heard it a few times this week alone.

I believe this other song out of her discography is a hidden gem, I'm putting you on with this classic.

HYPE ME UP

"Rave culture is a testament to the power of music and community, where strangers become friends, and the night becomes an unforgettable journey."

HYPE ME UP

Book that trip with your friends Ibiza, a captivating island nestled in the heart of the Mediterranean, beckons travelers from around the world with its irresistible blend of natural beauty and vibrant nightlife.

One cannot truly grasp the essence of Ibiza without experiencing its legendary club scene.

With world-renowned DJ sets, beachfront parties, and an electric atmosphere, Ibiza has earned its reputation as the ultimate party destination.

My core memories their will never be forgotten.

HYPE ME UP

Afrobeat, born from Africa's rhythms, resonates globally.

In recent years, to see the success of this Genre within the western countries such as the UK & US is so moving for many. We pray for the continuous success

The infectious beats, rich melodies, and potent messages transcend borders.

Celebrating life, addressing issues, and uniting people, Afrobeat is a joyous, powerful force. It embodies Africa's spirit, inspiring change and unity through music's timeless language.

HYPE ME UP

"Letting go of inhibitions is the first step towards discovering your limitless potential."

Think about that, & play this song.

HYPE ME UP

"To truly live, you must release the shackles of your inhibitions and embrace the beauty of spontaneity.

Take that as your will, life is about the memories, you can't take money with you."

HYPE ME UP

The emergence of Jungle music in the early 1990s revolutionized electronic music by blending break beats, reggae, and bass-heavy sounds.

This genre's frenetic rhythms and sub-bass frequencies laid the foundation for Drum & Bass, a faster, more complex evolution, pushing the boundaries of electronic music and captivating audiences worldwide.

This genre is the definition of how to get the blood flowing!

HYPE ME UP

Brazilian Funk, known for its infectious rhythms and provocative lyrics, has transcended its roots to captivate a global audience in recent years.

Its fusion of Afro-Brazilian beats and modern electronic elements resonates with diverse listeners, contributing to its widespread popularity and becoming a vibrant cultural export from Brazil to the world.

THE PAPER PLAYLIST: THE POWER OF MUSIC THERAPY

HYPE ME UP

"When work feels daunting, let the right tune be your secret weapon, turning even the mundane tasks into an exciting journey."

UK Garage will get you through!
The re-rise of the UKG excites me!
This means there will be a whole new generation of Garage heads & for that, I cannot wait.

Lets not forget this classic.

HYPE ME UP

The best pre-event ritual:
Crank up the music,
Let the beat move you,
Watch as it transforms you into a powerhouse of motivation and enthusiasm.

HYPE ME UP

"Just as an athlete warms up before a game, music is your mental warm-up, ensuring you're ready to perform at your best, whether at work or at the gym.

I cannot express to you in words, how much this song gets me going!

So scan the code & listen.

HYPE ME UP

There is nothing better than when a collaboration of two of the most influential biggest artists come together!

Music has this incredible power to elevate your spirits and ignite your energy, making it the ultimate chemical reaction for your brain!

HYPE ME UP

"I want you to know that, you will feel whole again,
its just a bad season, its not a bad life.. this too shall pass.

You will find a way back to yourself.

You can chose to be new today,
you can change your outlook,
your opinion,
the way you see yourself.

Its okay to cry & be sad, but don't stay stuck for too long.

Blast this song & dance!"

CHAPTER FIVE

IN MY FEELS, YEARNING FOR YOU.

"In the depths of our hearts,
we yearn for a love that
ignites our soul
and sets our spirit free."

IN MY FEELS, YEARNING FOR YOU.

"Like a symphony yearning for its perfect melody,
our hearts long to be united
in the dance of love"

IN MY FEELS, YEARNING FOR YOU.

"There's something so addictive about,
that toxic kind of love.

That low maintenance, easy connection... fuels the fire inside to keep you going.

You know you shouldn't, but its controllable."

IN MY FEELS, YEARNING FOR YOU.

"When I say I love you more, I don't mean I love you more than you love me. I mean I love you more than the bad days ahead of us, I love you more than any fight we will ever have, I love you more than the distance between us, I love you more than any obstacle that could try and come between us. I love you the most."

IN MY FEELS, YEARNING FOR YOU.

"In the garden of love, monogamy is the seed that flourishes into a lifetime of devotion.

Could you love until the end of time?"

IN MY FEELS, YEARNING FOR YOU.

"The yearning for love is a flame that keeps us warm in the coldest of nights.
My heart is yours, its you that I hold on too."

IN MY FEELS, YEARNING FOR YOU.

"There is always one person,
who will be engraved in your heart.
For good or bad, that person is a part of your chapter."

IN MY FEELS, YEARNING FOR YOU.

"Getting excited & waiting for them to text back, but trying to not show it, is the soft spot. "

Embrace this feeling & play this song.

IN MY FEELS, YEARNING FOR YOU.

"Between seas, galaxies and moons.
I was lucky I stepped on the same land.
I dreamed under the same stars as you."

IN MY FEELS, YEARNING FOR YOU.

Ask yourself, if you walked into a room with everyone you've ever met?

Who would you go looking for first?
- @peaeofdeace

IN MY FEELS, YEARNING FOR YOU.

"Now I have to remember you, for longer than I have known you" – C.C. Aurel

IN MY FEELS, YEARNING FOR YOU.

"Always Remember.
  Life is not about the breaths you take,
    it's the moments that
      take your breath away"

THE PAPER PLAYLIST: THE POWER OF MUSIC THERAPY

IN MY FEELS, YEARNING FOR YOU.

"Do you ever have that "What if?" person in your life?

All in good time, if not in this lifetime.. maybe the next."

IN MY FEELS, YEARNING FOR YOU.

"Remember the universe never says no,
it either says yes not now,
or I've got something better in store for you.

Every rejection is simply a redirection to the right person.

IN MY FEELS, YEARNING FOR YOU.

"Don't forget somewhere between hello & goodbye, there was love, so much love."

IN MY FEELS, YEARNING FOR YOU.

"Falling in love is like
opening your heart's window to the world,
letting vulnerability paint
the most beautiful scenery of your life."

IN MY FEELS, YEARNING FOR YOU.

"it's not the constant reassurance they'll stay, that can you put at ease.
Its not their texts or calls throughout the day, that can help you breathe.
My darling, its not their "I Love You" that can make you feel lovable.

For a long time, you've believed that your peace of mind and self-worth depend on how they treat you, and what they can do for you.

Its your reassurance that you're enough on your own. And their presence in your life adds to what you already have, that you need.

 Everything about this quote is correct.... but when you listen to this song – it all goes out the window.

IN MY FEELS, YEARNING FOR YOU.

"And I'd choose you; in a hundred lifetimes,
in a hundred worlds;
in any version of reality,
I'd find you & I'd choose you."

IN MY FEELS, YEARNING FOR YOU.

"Craving to intimately merge our souls,
our bodies yearn to script an eloquent symphony of passion

—a profound expression of desire that etches our love story in the fabric of time."

IN MY FEELS, YEARNING FOR YOU.

"Trapped somewhere between wanting to forget & wanting to hold on."

IN MY FEELS, YEARNING FOR YOU.

"Sexual chemistry with a soulmate ignites an intimate connection that transcends physical attraction.

It truly deepens emotional bonds,
fostering understanding,
trust, and a profound sense of oneness,
enriching the most beautiful,
soulful connection."

IN MY FEELS, YEARNING FOR YOU.

"One night I'll be saying 'I do' to a person that can read my mind too"

IN MY FEELS, YEARNING FOR YOU.

"If I could give you one thing in life,
I would give you the ability to see yourself through my eyes,

because only then you would realize
how special you are to me.

You are the only one who has ever been able to find me."

IN MY FEELS, YEARNING FOR YOU.

"Admire someone else's beauty,
without questioning your own."

THE PAPER PLAYLIST: THE POWER OF MUSIC THERAPY

IN MY FEELS, YEARNING FOR YOU.

"Like a fragile rose unfurling its petals in the morning sun,
love blossoms when vulnerability
is given the chance to bloom."

THE PAPER PLAYLIST: THE POWER OF MUSIC THERAPY

IN MY FEELS, YEARNING FOR YOU.

"Meeting you
was like listening to a song
for the first time,
knowing it would be my
favorite on the album."

THE PAPER PLAYLIST: THE POWER OF MUSIC THERAPY

IN MY FEELS, YEARNING FOR YOU.

"I am still silently hoping,
that time has made a mistake
and has already reserved a moment
for us to find each other again."

IN MY FEELS, YEARNING FOR YOU.

"In relationships,
we want people to value what we value, equally to what we value it.

That will never happen. What love is,
"I respect you so much for what you value, I actually respect that you are who you are because of what you value."

I don't want to change your values, if you want to change them. You don't love them."

THE PAPER PLAYLIST: THE POWER OF MUSIC THERAPY

IN MY FEELS, YEARNING FOR YOU.

"...enjoy the butterflies, enjoy being naïve, enjoy the nerves, the pressure, if you to stand on the top on day one, there's nothing to look forward too, enjoy the process of getting to know someone & fall in love. "

IN MY FEELS, YEARNING FOR YOU.

"Healing can be so hard,
when your inner child wants love,
your teenage self wants revenge,
your current self only wants peace."
- Charlamagne the God

This song you're about to hear has been embraced by so many. Some of the greatest artist in the world, the likes of Elton John, Mariah Carey, Lauryn Hill…

Most artists wish they wrote this masterpiece.

CHAPTER SIX

IN MY FEELS, F!*K YOU.

Don't make excuses for your ex, you cant put a flower in a arsehole and call it a vase.

IN MY FEELS, F!*K YOU.

"Being cheated on is like watching your favorite book being rewritten by someone else, with pages filled with lies and betrayal.", "In the symphony of love, being cheated on is the dissonant note that shatters the harmony of trust, leaving the heart to mourn."

"The scars of being cheated on are not visible, but they run deep, etching a painful reminder of the heart's vulnerability."

IN MY FEELS, F!*K YOU.

"Without rain, we wouldn't get flowers. Keep growing, the tears are just watering your soul. Let them go, move forward. You got this."

IN MY FEELS, F!*K YOU.

"Never underestimate, the power of my intuition. I can recognize your game, even before you play it. Mother f*%ker."

IN MY FEELS, F!*K YOU.

" Your happiness isn't found outside of yourself. Don't look for it from your other half. If your partner sucked that out of you, listen to this song. Karma's real."

THE PAPER PLAYLIST: THE POWER OF MUSIC THERAPY

IN MY FEELS,
F!*K YOU.

"Stop trying to to change people. If you're trying to change them. You don't love then you love their potential."

IN MY FEELS, F!*K YOU.

" What your attracted to when you're broken, disgusts you when you're healed.
Read that again & throw up the deuces."

IN MY FEELS, F!*K YOU.

"Start paying close attention to how you feel after you finish hanging out with someone or interacting with certain people.
Do you feel content?
        Happy?
                Full of energy?
                        Or do you feel just drained?

Some people will drain you without you being aware, but remember energy never lies.
Your body will let you know what is right for you & what is not. When you start paying attention, that not everyone at all deserves access to your energy or to you.

Not everyone deserves access to you."

IN MY FEELS, F!*K YOU.

"Replace "I should've known" with "now I know better." Forgive yourself, because self-shame is self-sabotage. Setting boundaries is hard. Being taken advantage of is harder."

IN MY FEELS, F!*K YOU.

"One day you're gonna be the best thing, someone ever took a chance on, I see it in you, the way you love, the way you hustle.. the way you carry yourself, you're not like the rest.

But instead you something different, something that's hard to find so when they find it, they make sure they take care of it."
- @WillKeepItReal

F**k them!

IN MY FEELS, F!*K YOU.

"You cant stop the waves, but you can learn to surf."

IN MY FEELS, F!*K YOU.

"Sometimes you gotta play the fool, to fool the fool. Who thinks they're fooling you."

IN MY FEELS, F!*K YOU.

"Old Keys, wont open new doors. Let them go." Play this song instead.

IN MY FEELS, F!*K YOU.

" If anyone is magically going to appear and just suddenly make your life better, just know that person is always going to be you."

- Brianna Taylor

Let this quote sit with you for a while. Don't give anybody else that power. You own that power & remind yourself if you ever doubt it.

IN MY FEELS, F!*K YOU.

" It never took much to love you. But it took everything I had to leave you."

IN MY FEELS, F!*K YOU.

"Stop allowing someone to show you twice, what they already showed you once."

IN MY FEELS, F!*K YOU.

"The woman who does not require validation from anyone is the most feared individual on the planet."
— Mohadesa Najumi

IN MY FEELS, F!*K YOU.

"You can still love someone **and still** choose to say goodbye to them. You can miss a person everyday **and still** be glad they're no longer in your life."

IN MY FEELS, F!*K YOU.

"You can do 99 things for some people, and all they will remember is the one thing you didn't do."

IN MY FEELS, F!*K YOU.

He said "Don't you feel lonely living in your own little world, she whispered

"don't you feel powerless, living in other peoples world."

IN MY FEELS, F!*K YOU.

Don't blame a clown for acting like a clown, instead ask yourself.. Why do you keep going to the circus?

IN MY FEELS, F!*K YOU.

Give yourself more credit.
You're trying to grow while trying to heal.
You're trying to forgive while trying to grieve.
You're trying to search while trying to let go.

On top of that, trying to love people whilst trying to love yourself. You're doing the best you can. – Vex King-

Enjoy life, that's how it supposed to be, living young & wild & free!

IN MY FEELS, F!*K YOU.

"I know what I can bring to the table, so trust me when I say.

I'm not afraid to eat alone."

I was sent this next song by my sister, whilst I was trying to get over an ex, who worked at the same place as me. I now cannot listen to this song without laughing.

IN MY FEELS, F!*K YOU.

"If someone's absence,
brings you peace.
You didn't lose anything."

IN MY FEELS, F!*K YOU.

"But the thing is, even if I could go back,
 I wouldn't belong there any more."

IN MY FEELS, F!*K YOU.

Too many people think the grass is greener, somewhere else.

But grass is green ..
..where you water it.

Remember that.

IN MY FEELS, F!*K YOU.

"Pay attention to who always can't with you, but can with everyone else."

IN MY FEELS, F!*K YOU.

Be the person who still tries.
After failure, after disappointment, after heartache, after exhaustion.

Just be the person who continues to show up...
Don't let anyone kill your vibe.

IN MY FEELS, F!*K YOU.

You haven't met all of the people you're going to love. You haven't traveled to your favorite place or made your favorite memories yet.

All of your best days are still ahead of you. Don't give up, your just getting started. F**k them!

CHAPTER SEVEN (8)

SUNDAY

"Sunday clear away the rust of the whole week." - Joseph Addison. So, pick up that sweeping brush, clear off those cobwebs & play this song loud!

SUNDAY

"Sundays are for cooking, for yourself & your loved ones. Make the best meal you've ever made.. yet.

SUNDAY

"Sunday is a day to relax, recharge, and let your soul catch up with your body.
Put that phone on do not disturb & tune into this.

THE PAPER PLAYLIST: THE POWER OF MUSIC THERAPY

SUNDAY

"Sunday is a reminder
 that you have the power
  to create a beautiful week ahead."

SUNDAY

"Sunday is the perfect day to do nothing or do everything! Whichever option you choose today, make sure after all is done. Close your eyes, rest your head & digest this beautiful song.

THE PAPER PLAYLIST: THE POWER OF MUSIC THERAPY

SUNDAY

"Today is a day to be grateful for all the little things in life that bring you joy. Get some air, get your favorite treat from your local store & play this song!

SUNDAY

"Sundays are like confetti floating in the air in slow motion, in the evening they reach the ground and you hope a bit of wind could blow on them so they could fly a bit longer." - Alain Bremond-Torrent

SUNDAY

"Sunday is the golden clasp that binds together the volume of the week." - Henry Wadsworth Longfellow.

What a way day to play one of the best songs ever written!

SUNDAY

"When faced with a week of adversity,
 find solace in the fact that
tomorrow is another day.
Offering a fresh to paint your world
with vibrant colors, this week."

SUNDAY

"Sunday is a gentle reminder that life is meant to be lived, not rushed.

Take it slow and savor every moment. "

THE PAPER PLAYLIST: THE POWER OF MUSIC THERAPY

SUNDAY

"Sunday is the day of the week when I am most likely to take the road less traveled." — Robert Frost

THE PAPER PLAYLIST: THE POWER OF MUSIC THERAPY

SUNDAY

Do you ever have a song, that takes you right back to a specific memory?

This song is one of those.

Where were you when you last heard it?

SUNDAY

Remember when you said.
  You needed to do a task, but never get around to it?

I know that feeling...
Get up, do a big deep clean of your house,
change those bed sheets & show respect
to yourself this Sunday.

Whilst doing you chores....sing through that broom stick
& play this song loud!

SUNDAY

There's something about listening to reggae, when you're cooking… that helps the flavor of your food.

Whats your favorite Sunday dinner?

SUNDAY

"Have a great Sunday! Experience life in all possible ways: good-bad, bitter-sweet, dark-light, summer-winter. Experience all the dualities. Don't be afraid of experience, because the more experience you have, the more mature you become." — Osho

SUNDAY

"Sunday is a time when you sit back and reflect on all the blessings that you have received.

Smile at all the good things that you are enjoying."— Sera Train

SUNDAY

Its not about "having" time.

It's about making time for your people that means the most.

This Sunday is the right time.

THE PAPER PLAYLIST: THE POWER OF MUSIC THERAPY

SUNDAY

A Feel Good Sunday, would not be feel good without a 90s R&B Classic.

If you know, you know.....

SUNDAY

If you can count on one hand, the amount of people who are dear to you.

 Count yourself lucky.

Spend a this Sunday together.

Cause' you don't know what you got 'till its gone.

SUNDAY

    2 parents, 4 Grandparents, 8 great-grandparents, 16 great-great-grandparents, 32 third great-grandparents, 64 fourth great-grandparents, 128 fifths-great grandparents, 256/ sixth great-grandparents, 512 sevenths great-grandparents, 1024 eighths great-grandparents , 2048 nineth great-grandparents.
For you to be born today.

    From 12 previous generations, you needed a total of 4094 ancestors over the last 400 years. Think for a moment how any struggles,
how many battles, how many difficulties, how much sadness, how much happiness, how many love stories, how many expressions of hope for the future, did your ancestors have to undergo, for you to exist in this world?

Use this day for yourself.

There is only one song, I can end this book on & dedicate to you personally... Enjoy

Welcome to the end of the book.

Please ensure to pick up this book, whenever you need to remind yourself how incredible you are, do some self healing or just listen to some absolute Bangers!

Have you ever had a "full circle" moment with a song?

Did you scan the front cover?

A little secret…

This song was my reason to write this book.

Sometimes, some things are better left unsaid.

Let the music play

Thanks for reading, until next time.